Monarchs to Mexico

by Isabella Cummings
illustrated by Christine Joy Pratt

Cover art by Lynn Titleman

Printed in the United States of America

ISBN 0-15-317266-5 – Monarchs to Mexico

Ordering Options
ISBN 0-15-318633-X (Package of 5)
ISBN 0-15-316986-9 (Grade 2 Package)

3 4 5 6 7 8 9 10 179 02 01 00

It was early fall in North America. At the zoo, the leaves had begun to change color. Spectators came to the zoo to see both the changing leaves and the animals.

As the days grew colder, the giraffes and elephants moved inside. The polar bears, however, refused to use their indoor homes. They stood their ground outdoors because they liked the cold.

Like the polar bears, many spectators
were outside, too. The spectators also
stood their ground against the cold. They
refused to let cold weather stop them from
enjoying the zoo.

High in the bright sky, a huge group of monarch butterflies flew over the zoo. The North American winter would be too cold for them. They were off to find hospitality in a warmer place.

4

Some of the monarch butterflies were only two or three weeks old. But these young heroes and heroines were performing a feat that many animals could not. They were making a trip to Mexico. The butterflies liked the warmer hospitality of the Mexican mountains.

Making this migration was quite a feat. Some of the butterflies had to travel more than 1,500 miles.

As the monarch butterflies flew south, others joined them in their migration to Mexico. How many monarchs were in the sky now?

The butterflies flew about fifty miles
every day. Then they stopped to rest.
Some landed on tree branches. Others
landed on flowers.

8

The butterflies ate nectar from
flowers. It is hard to believe, but these
butterflies gained weight during their
flight! The fat in their bodies gave them
energy to fly. The strong winds helped in
their flight, too.

After many weeks, more than one hundred million monarch butterflies arrived in the Mexican mountains. Some of the butterflies returned to the same trees they had lived in the year before!

10

The butterfly heroes and heroines were happy and warm. Far to the north, there were cold winds and snow. In the Mexican mountains, it was cool but not cold. It was perfect for the monarchs.

The monarch butterflies would stay in Mexico for five or six months. When spring arrived, they would make another amazing trip. They would travel back to their northern homes!

Monarch Butterfly Facts

On a sheet of paper, write the numbers 1 to 8. Read the sentences in the butterfly. If the sentence tells something true, write a *T*. If the sentence tells something not true, or false, write an *F*. (Turn the page to find the answers.)

1. Some monarch butterflies migrate when they are just two or three weeks old.

2. Monarch butterflies fly north when it gets cold.

3. Monarch butterflies can fly fifty miles in one day.

4. Many monarch butterflies travel to Mexico every year.

5. The wind helps the monarch butterflies fly.

6. Monarch butterflies lose weight when they travel to Mexico.

7. Monarch butterflies get energy from their fat.

8. Monarch butterflies eat nectar.

School-Home Connection Invite your child to read Monarchs to Mexico to you. Then ask your child to tell you three facts he or she learned about monarch butterflies.

TAKE-HOME BOOK
Just in Time
Use with "Ruth Law Thrills a Nation."